FINALLY NAKED

Written By:
Tresa Simmons

TABLE OF CONTENTS

DEDICATION

I dedicate this book to my daughters, Latonya, Asunia, Delores, and Mae, and my sons, Esaias and Antonio. I willed for a better life and to be a better person because all of you were worth it. I dedicate this book to my mom who gave me life and all the women everywhere who believed in me. Some of you planted seeds; some of you watered; some of you pulled up the weeds; some of you picked the fruit. Nevertheless, all of you contributed to me being the woman I am today.

To every woman, I rise and pussy-soar for all of us.

I dedicate this book to my inner guru, Little Tresa, for her strength, fortitude, determination, courage, tenacity, passion, fire, and her spunk. You fought for me when I should have been taking care of you.

Thank you.

1

FOREWORD

By: Janine Ingram

We are in a time of great awakening on this planet. An awakening of the feminine presence on the planet. The light of truth, intensifying with each passing moment, is nudging many to step forward and share what they know. However, that journey to our personal awakening requires full use of spirit-nourishing tools. These tools that you have in your spiritual toolbox are important companions for your personal transformation.

I am amazed as I watch Tresa L. Simmons become the architect of her life using her spiritual tools of meditation, prayer, journaling, forgiveness, love, gratitude, and womb work. I have watched her re-invent herself, embracing her feminine energy, understanding who she is in Christ Consciousness, and recognizing the gift she is to this earth. This mind shift transformation takes work, and it is reflected in her actions and behavior, not to mention how she treats herself tri-dimensionally, meaning mind, body, and spirit.

My name is Janine A. Ingram, also known as The Love Goddess or Lady Love. Tresa has been a part of my Art of Sexual Magic workshops, and watching her use her sexual energy to heal, not to mention building her relationship with her body, is beyond amazing. I use a variety of tools, including breath, meditation, and talk therapy to guide people into an expanded experience to access pleasure points in the body while moving that pleasure or energy up through the body or chakras, bringing that powerful energy through the chakra system and transforming that energy to materialize the original intentions.

This growth has impacted Tresa in ways she probably cannot imagine. In the passages that follow, Tresa takes ownership of her personal power. Her poetry demonstrates how she walks flawlessly through life. It is in the way she flaunts her Divine Feminine because she knows she's got it. She makes no apologies because she is comfortable in her own skin. She takes extreme self-care because she honors her body as the Divine temple of the Creator. Wanting to share what she has learned, through her writings, she shows the reader how to do the same. You will see her coming with her head held high and a confident smile parting her beautiful lips. She has given voice to her truth. She now knows that she is an instrument of love, also understanding that life is graced by her presence, and that she is a joy in motion.

Watching Tresa step into her purpose is an inspiration for all women! It reminds me of what my grandmother used to say, "Baby, purpose gave life to you; you did not give life to purpose." With that being said, thank you, Tresa, for stepping into your calling and reminding us that the Most High has promised to provide, to protect, to answer, and to always be with us. As you read the words that have been given to Tresa L. Simmons in this birthing project from the Universe *Finally Naked! My Almost 60-Year Journey to Self-Acceptance,* may you find yourself getting naked. A naked that will have you journey into an inner space of your own self-acceptance.

INTRODUCTION

I have always loved to read and to write. But it was not until the summer of 2017 that I was introduced to three beautiful women who were connected by their purpose in life. Each in their own way pointed me in the direction of the light and nudged me to keep walking. I met Ber-Henda Williams at Transforming Love Community, who introduced me to Reshoun Foster, who introduced me to Imani Williams, an administrator for the "Writers – Black Art Connected" Group. Imani listened when I said someday I wanted to write a book. She suggested I join the group. As we say, the rest is history.

I had no idea that poetry would lead me back to myself, but it did in an epiphany style awakening. As I look over my poetry, something I do from time to time, I see my writings were a diary of my evolution that came to me in masterful ways. I was often meeting aspects of myself that only my psyche could receive in this manner. I had to be open and become non-attached to the outcome of how my prayers were answered. I remember praying really hard and long while crying for freedom, even when I had no clue what it was, how it would show up, or the price it would cost me. Being aware of the role poetry has played in my life in the course of 3 years is fascinating as I observe my journey to self-acceptance.

My journey to self-acceptance has been an adventure, to say the least, but not always fun and often downright painful. The poetry in this book was chosen because it gave me clues that led me back to my center. A center that had been obliterated through trauma and pain starting very early in my life. I was distracted and disconnected from my own mind, soul, and body. My emotions were tattered. It was my soul that held the broken pieces and the answers and the questions. The poems returned the pieces of myself to their rightful place in the most gentle and loving way possible. I had to lean into my process and let it flow. It is my prayer that you will find this true as well. My writings are not written in any kind of order other than in categories.

CHAPTER 1:

FREE STYLING

Free Styling, for me, is about allowing what wanted to flow through me uninhibited to do so. Often a melody of words that I could not or would not have allowed to proceed in their purest form had I been wrapped in my head came through. My soul was dictating to me what was below the surface of my traumas as well as the best parts of me that I would become reacquainted with. Many times I look back only to marvel at my process and to see when my Higher Self took over.

* * * * * *

My Expression is the woman I am and the woman I will be. She is clear about who and what she chooses to be. She is transparent and naked.

Alive is more than the beating of my heart. It is about acknowledging and respecting consciousness that is my energetic rhythm.

Words, the Lover of My Soul, is a message that writing is my salvation. It is a huge clue on my magical journey. My poetry tells my story from pain and chaos to redemption, freedom, and pleasure.

I have a fascination with pole dancing. I seriously want to learn. It is something about the pole that screams liberty … no self-consciousness allowed. *Riding the Pole* was inspired by this desire.

Brown Eyes downloaded in me after I took a picture and looked into my eyes—they were no longer brown but grey. Healing was expressing in my body. I truly believe that as we heal, it is possible for our DNA to change forms.

MY EXPRESSION

Wolf wild

Intuition on fleek

Third eye ready

Goddess dancing in rhythm with the moon

Oceans swaying in her vein

Living out loud

Dancing in color

Unapologetic

Pussy popping

Swirls of essence

A worshipped woman with no walls

Boundaries be damned

PULSE

Authentic

Fully Alive

Living

Being

Pulsating

My energetic heartbeat

WORDS, THE LOVER
OF MY SOUL

You are the lover of my soul

A description of what makes me whole

Describing those yes, those before a period,
comma, semi-colon, and exclamation mark

Those phrases, words, sentences that signal
punctuations that lead or say park

I dig for you like gold

My God, my treasure! YOU, WORDS, are the
lover of my soul that even I can't measure

While you wrap me like a man, his woman,
his lover, you keep lecturing me to come
from under the cover

You say you have me and hold me tight

You say you yourself are the words
that will keep my soul right

Whether in the morning, noonday, or at night,
you tell me surrender and let go of the fight

For YOU, WORDS, the lover of my soul,
were sent here to take me deeper,
wider, and make me whole

You say to me of yourself, I am a gift.
Unwrap me. Words untouched, tap into me

Tap into me, tap into me

I am that road map that leads you to places you
have never seen, but you will come fast and hard
as if an orgasm; you scream in your dream

Just let me make love to you
as the lover of your soul

You will never regret the power that I hold

I will let you taste of me as I set you free

I am the lover of your soul

In words, phrases, sentences come to make your
life whole

I am given different meanings by many so
numerous they call me good and plenty

Yet I choose you among the many and the few

Make love to me in words, phrases, sentences,
and paragraphs; I got you

Don't you feel my emotions, tears,
laughter, pain, happiness, and joy?

I know you see me, feel me, hear me, so stop
picking me up, putting me down like a toy

I will give you bliss that is powerful and new

Please if you do not embrace me,
I can make you blue

So please hear me when I say
I am the lover of your soul

In words, phrases, sentences,
I mesmerize you to make you whole

RIDING THE POLE

I step to you as you stand at attention

Hands on hips

Legs wide

Me looking and smiling from side to side

My hair big, denoting my glory

I look at you and say it is time to tell our story

I think of riding you now, honoring our treasure

Damn, our experiences are too deep to measure

But I will try

Treasure of rubies, Garnet stones, black
diamonds, and jewelry untold

I feel so juicy standing relentlessly transparent as
this poem unfolds

Flowing in my experiential DNA

All mixed up with my healthy
ability to love and play

It is not always easy as I learned you

Soft and hard touches

Long and short brushes

Hugs

Legs open oh so right

Legs shut oh so tight

Up I rode you and down again

I even gave you a twirl and a spin

You never betrayed me or let me down

You just stood at attention
as I went round and round

I see you look at me as I look at the pole

Your stare tells it all

Mouth open wide

I wink and whisper, "Close
it before a fly goes inside!"

You squint and move oh so slow

Before I know it, your hands are in the flow

I imagine you are reminded
of how I ride this pole

I smile, and I think two sessions in one

I schooled your ass

And cum, you did, as you watched me tell my story of my pole dancing class

BROWN EYES

I see with new eyes, and they
say freedom has changed me

As I look closer, what do I see?

Brown eyes from birth, or was that an illusion?

Today, I take a closer look, and gray is the choice
of my new life choosing

No, I never said change eyes from brown to gray

However, you saw fit my
body to rearrange my DNA

Maybe it is me bugging

But as I lean in, I remember,
brown eyes now turned gray

CHAPTER 2:

LIFE

The poems in this section tell the story of duality and the wrestling that happened within me. I wrestled with the light and shadow parts of myself, seeing one as better, and making one worse. That is like accepting my foot with no blemish and despising the one with a blemish. Both feet are needed as is, both my light and shadows. The poetry in this section reveals my struggles. These struggles were preparing me in spite of the hardships, heartaches, chaos, and pain. A beautiful lotus flower made it through the mud. It took self-acceptance to embrace all of me.

* * * * * *

A Conversation with My Younger Self is about her letting me know how she felt. I would ask my inner child what she had to say. I would never have heard the depth of her heart and seen her experiences through her eyes except through the art of poetry as given to me because I lived in my head at that time. Mini-me let me know she suffered at my hands, but she never gave up on me. I realize that initially, it was men that unlawfully took from me. Over a period of time, I became those men. Unbeknownst to me, I had taken on the identity of my abusers. I picked up where they left off. I was self-destructive … until I wasn't. I am not my past nor the men.

Ancestors Calling and Redemption is the sounding of an alarm for me to reconnect to my emotions and my feelings. I am compelled to remember I always have the support of my ancestors, whether on this side of the veil or the other. My passion is the best fuel for my emotions and my feelings. All emotions need to be accepted. All have value.

Loving Someone Who Cannot Love You Back tells of a time in my life when Spirit had to remind me that it is I who was fighting for my own limitation keeping me broken and unable to take flight. This can lead to depression, anger, anxiety, stress, or other emotions. *Acceptance* is about inviting my emotions in to converse with them and asking my feelings to have a seat at the table as I wait for them to tell me what they need, else the knock at the door will get louder. They want to be heard, acknowledged, and expressed. The lesson is all about surrender and understanding that joy and pain are equal teachers and both are needed.

Black Woman tells of a woman who is an over giver and is not appreciated.

A CONVERSATION WITH MY YOUNGER SELF

I see it now, you holding on like
a door on its last hinge

Crying, screaming, and raging
eyes at them but at me

I see you, said you, after all these
men took like on a drunken binge

They kept coming back for more all the while I
was screaming for you to see my ability to restore

We were broken pieces torn apart from greed and
lust of what was not theirs to have

But I was there to help you to abort the pain

However, your mindset in agreement
with them had become one of self-abuse
as you said, "Let it rain!"

You did not deserve this treatment, and I was
trying to free us both, as we were like one bird
with two broken wings

I finally understand Maya's poem
I Know Why the Caged Bird Sings

I was your younger self walking on broken glass

And you, my friend, were
the worst kicking your own ass

Your pain would not allow you
to see you had a friend in me

Today, we merge victorious me strong and at
rest, experiencing peace at its best

No more crying, not just for what I saw
you go through, but also because you
now understand I was there for you

You were never alone, and I took care of you …
as best I could … like a shoe that was too little
for my feet, I took on a role I was definitely
unequipped to meet

I love you, but I like you more

The woman you have grown into
no longer needs to keep score

Instead, you have merged with your
younger self me, and we are happy

No more living from broken pieces

Now living our lives in the roots of wholeness

Being restored and remade in Spiritual Boldness

I would not change nothing for my journey;
although I did not feel that way then

Happier times are upon us because you
took time to help me see within

I am your younger self. I am you

I see you; the strength you embody
is you, the epitome of power

Power in all stages and phases of a mental
shift, from brokenness to "I am the shit;
don't fuck with me. I am a bad bitch!"

As your younger self, I get to take a seat, enjoy
my place, while you reign supreme, making no
apology for taking up space

We did not understand that to gather all of the
scattered pieces was part of the plan

What did I know? I was as immature as I was
young, but I held on tight to those pieces like a
door on its last hinge

Unable to stop men from taking
on their sexual binge

The last laugh is ours, a gift of our strength
unknown … at the time

A powerful merge of our younger and older souls

Unfolding as

The gathering of our pieces is
our story now being told

ANCESTORS CALLING

I see you from afar

No face but a haze

Yet I knew you as that shining star

It feels like a maze

As I walk to the light

So numb

From this energetic fight

My plight

Dumming down, playing dumb

As the walking dead

No pulse

Freedom calling my name

Thawing me out

Is it your scream or mine

calling for the blood of emotions to awaken?

Please forgive me; I had mistaken

feelings as my enemy

Not feeling is killing me

It is my ancestors I see

Screaming

Don't play

Our blood did not fall

for you to play small

Feel the pull

We are here to guide you

REDEMPTION

Feel the power instilled in you
before your inception

You are born and reborn

Again and again and again

Yet nothing changes your miraculous conception

Ideas of divine prayers said over you

The ability to feel, sense, and intuit your way

In the cosmos of our University

Of intentional and purposeful diversity

Liquid tears, belly laughs,
orgasms of mental stimulation

The why of many a migration

Back to themselves to feel what
they have known to be true

from the moment they were born

Yet torn

by man's idea that feelings are for the weak

when in reality they are the safety we seek

Allow yourself to return to the womb

For your death clothes emotions
wrapped in a tomb

Will become her sanctuary

The dead do arise as the Phoenix from the ashes

Stretch your hands and bless her as
she takes you into a journey

The colors of the rainbow on fire

Causing you to spit your desire

Formulated in your emotions,
senses, and feelings

LOVING SOMEONE WHO CANNOT LOVE YOU BACK

You see

I thought it was the outside
world that had forgotten me

But nooo

It was I

Emotionally immature

Bankrupt

Keeping Score

Zero, zero, zero

Corrupt

Hijacking my own sanity and peace

Disgracing my space

Telling my body it's too

You name it

I did not want to claim it …

My beauty

My own reflection …

My greatness

As I fought for my own limitation

My spirit grounded

Too heavy to fly

Carrying tears

of a grieved Soul

Loving me who could not love her back

ACCEPTANCE

There you are again, your invisibility
pulling at me so strong

That deep connection of seeming perfection

Why did I feel something was wrong?

Your knocks have been gentle nudges,
loud bangs, and sometimes cold
fog seeping through my pores

Your insurrection is a much deeper
connection than I have allowed

I surrender

Sometimes they call you depression;
other times anguish, sorrow, and pain

But you bring a lesson through my
experiences that keep calling out my name

You say I must learn them, and I ask teach me

I rolled out the royal treatment
as the alchemical woman I am

Preparing to feel my way through
blazing hot sand, cold winter nights,
autumn retreats, and spring dances

Observing from afar the mask of
broken pieces of shattered dreams

My religion once was the invisibility of my
divisibility, constantly adding, multiplying,
dividing, and finally subtracting myself

My Yes to you was a vibrational match,
a sacred key setting off an instantaneous
eclipse shifting cosmic alignment

Then and only then did I accept your
place in the room at the table

You, my instructor, brought the knowledge
that joy and pain are equal teachers

In expectance of your arrival

I swept away the cobwebs of lies

Even the lingering doubt that I have to strive

Striving to rid you of your voice

Striving to rid you of your choice … to choose me

As you communicate the essence of my strength

You are a guidepost a travel map, a new direction

I am open for healing salve of correction

Sometimes it feels as if you are
a bully coming on too strong

But you whisper my resistance is
keeping me from being free

When I finally invited you in, you sat
beside happiness, laughter, and poise

Taking your rightful place,
you brought on the noise

Your temperament and the cacophony
of your rhythm for my life

Feels like I am freezing while naked in the winter

Or drowning in the bed of hell

Yet I am told that in both

My soul is whispered to

Magic happened in my surrender

I am always the culmination of the
ACCEPTANCE of owning my
shadows and my light

BLACK WOMAN

I've heard it said that black
women like roses have thorns

Prickly and painful

Sharpened by hurts they have born

BEHOLD

There is beauty in their pain
adorned in love as they stand tall

Crowned in thorns and all

Cursed by the men they birth

Still, she reaches past her pain
to hold space for their worth

Sometimes they say the black woman ain't shit

The dichotomy of their foolish
words is mind-boggling

The contrast is too deep too wide

This has not stopped the black
woman from setting her tears aside

Allowing herself to have union
with you, black man

Becoming pregnant with her dreams and yours

Bending her back, saying step up so you can soar

While her dreams remain in Never Never Land

Lending you her two hands

Two feet, her sleep, her peace, and her identity

Yet you call her prickly and sharp
as the thorn on a rose

If she has become these things, it is a testament

Your ignorance and pride
won't allow you to honor the truth

Nor give space for black women to be other

A beautiful rose of various shades and colors

A dichotomy of all her experiences

CHAPTER 3:

SEXUAL HEALING

I often smile when I get to talk about sexual healing because it is deeper than two people fucking or having sex. It is an intimate encounter with another that does not necessarily have anything to do with sexual penetration. It is about opening up to an experience where we get to see a glimpse of heaven and understand the bliss that Goddess must have made creating us in an intimate way that only she could have. Sexual healing opens up a creative space, and orgasms can happen anywhere as we learn to make love to our words, our food, ourselves, our man or women, and the world. Orgasmic living is juicy and sacred living. This is deeply rewarding for me, a far cry from the year-old girl two weeks shy of her birthday being touched by her stepfather.

There is a huge space from being an actor in my life to being the lead director.

* * * * * *

Ironically, one of the first poems that I wrote was *Offering*. Offerings are initiated upon my body (altar). The greatest offering is owning my desire for pleasure and giving myself permission to have it. *A Safe Space* is about people using the magic and beauty of lovemaking, consciously choosing to heal each other and speak life rather than against each other. *Being Made Love To* speaks to the power of our imagination.

OFFERING

Self-pleasuring is my offering to this body

Sanctified by my touch

Revered by the most Holy I AM

Me

A SAFE SPACE

You could lay in it and savor it for as long as you want. You could taste my flowing juices and drink from my sweet, sweet nectar. You could suckle my breast dipped in honey and feed me bananas, strawberries, and grapes. Your voice, your conversation make me have a womb-blowing orgasm that shoots through me like the birthing of our togetherness formed in oneness of forgiveness and love.

I would return your love and lovemaking unconditionally, unbridled, and untamed. I would be the priestess to your priest nature, the moon to your sun, and light for your shadows.

My tears from your good loving would heal the scrapes and scratches and the deep wounds we have caused each other in our carelessness. Neither would give a damn about being right. We have chosen to set our house to free our minds and our souls as we liberate ourselves through the healing motion of the pussy formed and shaped a safe space for you.

BEING MADE LOVE TO

I feel you caressing my face oh so gently. Kissing my lips with your warmth while making a path between my twins as they reach to taste you.

Ahhhh, continuing on your journey to take a dip in my navel and kiss me there only to keep flowing over my lotus petal, making her moans reach the heavens.

Fuck, she thinks she is seeing heaven in a glimpse, or maybe it's the angels. I see you, or should I say I feel your power as you go between the folds of my flower.

Ooooweee, yes, I like you there where you mix with my juices already forming because I am turned on by you. While simultaneously caressing your way down the center of my back. Damn, you feel so erotic.

I can tell you are passionate about me. Your path is forceful, and you are going straight to the point. You continue to make your way through the crack of my ass where you, too, meet up with

my juices that have been mixed with
your power from the front to the back.

I scream at the feeling of being loved and touched
in such a generous way. You are not putting
out the fire but increasing it. How can this be?
It must be magic. It has to be magic!!

The fire in me burns as "you water" empowers it
to a greater spark as you both dance and play
with my imagination.

CHAPTER 4:

EMPOWERED WOMAN

I do not know if there is anything more exhilarating than being an empowered woman. To walk with confidence is powerful, but to take that walk inward and rock it, knowing this is your world, and you can create it however you like, is even more formidable. To my delight, when I saw poetry of this magnitude being written, not at first but later, I came to understand my evolution.

* * * * * *

My Truth is a set of beautiful adjectives in motion that describe me. I'm giddy, as I have become an observer of how my soul describes me. **A Soul Come Alive** and **I Dance** are indescribable. I am in motion.

43

I'm Seducing is a heartfelt peace for me. I feel like I have been given a formula, and writing this is a reminder the feminine can woo and bring anything to herself, even herself, if done correctly. I am teasing and seducing the best parts of myself as I let go of the judgments, should haves, could haves, and just be and allow. *What Would I Be without the Judgments* expresses so poignantly what transpires when I see myself without discrimination.

MY TRUTH

I AM

Expression

Laughter

Freedom

Love

Shakti Divine

I AM shockingly creamy, healthy, organic, and delightfully delicious

Phenomenal woman

Worshipped woman

Witch woman

Medicine woman

Extremely magical woman

I AM sexy brilliance

Bodaciously bold

Creatively fulfilled

I AM a rare hussy of imagination

Funny ... x-tra fun

Eccentric and spicy to delight

Intensely beautiful

A pearl of sensuality

Sexual energy rising

Alchemical Evolution

A woman gone wild

Untamable

Living my best life

A SOUL COME ALIVE

I feel like howling at the moon

A reflection of the energy of the feminine

Inside of me

Rays of light on the backdrop
of darkness looking out

My light creating space for the
darkness to explore herself

Within

My moon guides the night into morning

I'm almost there

Unfurling, unbending, standing in all my glory

A moon Goddess of oneness with all things

An integrated woman of truth

A Soul come alive

I am the best of my experiences

I DANCE

I dance to the music of the Divine Feminine

Seduction lies in my pelvis
gyrating to her language

Snake arising, teasing my senses

Creating Laughter

A symphony of beats that keeps me alive

I AM SEDUCING

I AM seducing

Myself in the open

My dreams into my visions in real time

My conversations to voice nothing but praise on
this beautiful black sister honoring her

I AM seducing

My intention … making love to it and creating
purposeful living

My womb, as she holds stories that are ready to
be told, first preparing me to listen

My pussy with its crystals, diamonds,
gold, and silver linings charming her
as she teaches me the sacredness of
receiving and the power she has to give

I AM seducing

My legacy as I lean into the strength of my
ancestors

My senses as they lead me to further touch the
deepest part of me turning my sexuality into fire

My sexy leading me into intimate
moments with myself with my clothes on

Myself as I become the offering on my altar rising
free of guilt and shame

WHAT WOULD I BE WITHOUT THE JUDGMENT?

Answer: I AM

I AM …

Light and free

Poetry in motion with...

No rhyme or reason

Happiness, joy, peace, love wrapped in laughter

Bowing down to my own significance

Authentic

Beauty in the vortex

Colors and energy of bright reds, oranges, greens, yellows, pinks, blues

Nurtured by my own breast

Healing words and flowers

I AM

The power of masturbation in real time

A climax of passion in my daily life called Tresa

Entering into a praise of energetic vibration

Connection of heart

A salutation

Humble

Thankful

Gratitude is my Strength

Powerful

Playing in space that has no time

I AM

The call of the Siren for the Feminine Divine

The vortex of my womb that
meets my Yoni in Yes

I AM

The sun and the moon in motion lighting my way

Singing in cacophony with
the rain and the thunder

The rainbow and the wind

The trees and the seed

I AM

More than enough

A statement of my greatness

I AM

Brilliant

Phenomenal

Ancestors beating the drum

I AM Uniquely ME

CHAPTER 5:

US

I'm a goddess but not just any goddess. I am a worshipped woman, the Priestess of Pleasure. I write about what was, what is, and what will be because my Soul is an expression of all three. Moment by moment, my present becomes my past, and my future becomes my now. Time is collapsing as I see you, my Beloved.

* * * * * *

As in any relationship, there are challenges including a woman who does not know her worth, so no matter what her partner says or tells her, she does not believe him. *Call My Name* captures this truth beautifully. There was a time it did not matter what a man said, I could not hear him. *My Reality* tells of my experience of self-betrayal to myself. **Tears on My Pillar** (Co-written by Montego Ware) speaks of a crush I had on a married man that I walked away from. I never fulfilled it, but it was difficult. Difficult only because I was still looking for love in the wrong places, and for me, that was men who were unavailable emotionally. In this case, it was physically as well.

In *Your Life*, one's partner wonders if he is going crazy because he is drawn to honor her in every way. *I Saw You Today* reminds me that if we look for love, we will always find it. *Imagination Running Wild* tells the story of magnetism and fascination for a man that occurs in my dreams. *Too Freaky* is a poem of sexual freedom and a woman who is demanding hers.

YOUR LIFE

I walked into the room today

Victory in my hips and thighs

Manifesting pleasure and delight in my stride

Telling a story with momentum

I had no words for

I looked up

Your smile celebrated me

Before you fell to your knees

Metaphorically

I see your chuckle turn from
a slow walk into a jog

Into laughter leading you to question your sanity

You should

For this has become your life

CALL MY NAME

I said call my name, and you said Love.

I said I'm waiting for you to call
my name, and you said Peace.

I asked again, call my name,
and you said Solitude.

I looked, and my facial expression
said call my name. You said Laughter.

Tears rolled. I needed you to see me.
I screamed call my name. You said I have.

I SAW YOU TODAY

I saw you today

In the smile of the being standing next to me

Happiness takes many shapes and forms

I smelled you today

In the trees, the flowers, and in my own laughter

Your aroma of happiness knows no boundaries

I tasted you today

In my joy, my peace, and in the rain

I open wide, and you slid easily down my throat

I felt your touch today

Your sunshine reached me from afar

You played my senses

My taste buds awakened … the warm mellow
of honey laced in cinnamon and peaches

I saw you today in all that I did

I DRINK YOU IN

From the moment I laid eyes on you,

Your shade of brown captivated me

From your brown orbits shaped in kindness

To your brown skin draped in warmness

To the strength of your arms … sinews of power

Hmmm I drink you in

So delicious

I watch you smile and see white against the
brown backdrops

I see your brown lips moving, and I hear words

Unable to comprehend your utterance

I'm in a trance

Hmmm I drink you in

So fulfilling

I drink in the essence of your laughter

The funny of your bone

Bone reality that your shade of
brown is making me thirsty

Hmmm I drink you in

Tasting my own aphrodisiac

My thirst is quenched as I drink
in your shade of brown

Hmmmm, ahhhhh, I drink you in

Not wanting to share you

In my mind, I box up the tall
handsome glass of juicy delight

My reality

I can't help it

You leave a sweet taste in my mouth as
I catch the last drip of you with my tongue

TEARS ON MY PILLAR

Love, don't let the silver band
on my left finger taunt you

Or distract your conscience from
me declaring, "I want you!"

I've married and known all over Seattle;
otherwise, I'd flaunt you

But in the darkness, I'm like the
drowsiness that comes upon you

Dreams of you hidden in my imagination

Shadows of temptations

Of a married man who makes me want to bend
time and rewind when he said, "I do!"

This time, I'm gonna give
you something so potent

That it's not interrupted when your eyes open

From the feel of your shapely lips against mine

You're tempted to continue the kissing game we
played to unwind ...

Sigh

This is fucked up; a reality

I cannot change except in my dream

My lips suck you back into the dream by your
tongue

As my hands strut up and down your right
forearm

Our energies keep the temptation steady

You're not ready to leave something
so sensual yet calm, are you?

I cry, yet I dare not allow

The beauty of your touch

A flutter of my heart as

Temptations mirror the beauty of butterflies

Who stay when their very survival
of my freedom lies in taking flight

Please stay out of my dreams, leaving
my wings heavy this black night

I leave the imprint of my love as I awaken
to my pillow wet with my pain

MY REALITY

We started out with the moon high in the sky

With me stopping in to say goodbye

No, you didn't know

But as I looked at you

Thoughts ran through my mind as I said to
myself one more time

We made love through the night

I lost my urgency to stop the flow

The flow of my blood mingled
with your poisonous darts

Lodged in my broken and damaged heart

Don't you remember? You put them there

She, me, us

Times like now I, too, forget … until

I ask the question

Besides the moans and screams
becoming louder in my head in this bed,

What has changed?

Not a damn thing

Not even our reality

IMAGINATION RUNNING WILD

My wildest imagination was never a
match for the depth of your eyes nor
the beauty of your smile

Definitely not the intensity of your gaze

I stared back

I knew you

You are the man in my dreams

Standing before me

Skin the color of midnight

Arms in my mind reaching for me, holding
me like the night before the dawn

I knew you

I wonder, do you remember me to

I listened as you spoke

I heard that voice before

But still, nothing prepared me for the melodic

Words you imparted, tasting like sweet
honey cones dripping in syrup

Preparing me a path that only Queens walk

I knew you

We danced in meadows

Played in the rain

Took long walks in the park

Dipped our bodies in poetry

Leaving trails of words and sounds
multiplied and created more of the same

I knew you

Do you remember me

Now

A perfect gentleman

A King

A man of honor

And I, a perfect lady

But not in my wildest imaginations

TOO FREAKY

I heard you, too freaky, huh …

Well, freaky enough to suck your dick when you
open your legs wide and say swallow

Too freaky when I say taste me
and take me to paradise

Well, freaky enough to ask me to turn
over or bend while you penetrate my ass

Too freaky when I ask for kisses,
which you say you do not do

Freaky enough to ask me to ride
you till ou scream "oh fuck"

Too freaky to take time for me to
experience ecstasy of your making

I pretended that it was OK, at least in
my head. My emotions tell me I am
angry when you say to me I desire too freaky sex.

You have no idea, and maybe that is best. The
things I have in my mind, you would send me to
jail for.

I release you and your too freaky judgments of my sexual preferences. But I say shhhh … listen …

Listen, listen, be still and listen. What you didn't do, he did. Do you hear the sighs, moans, and screams when he ate me like I was the best tasting cream on the planet, when he kissed me until I could not catch my breath, and when he fucked me until my cumming triggered his own? Too freaky for you … for him ... shhhhhh, just listen.

CHAPTER 6:

SHORT LOVE STORIES IN POETRY

Short stories written as poetry is intimacy between a man and a woman. As these poems began to unfold, I later understood how much my sexual freedom has manifested itself. It's a beautiful expression of sexual sovereignty. It takes the strength, boldness to honor one's autonomy to master self-love, sensuality, and sexuality. I co-wrote these poems with Montego Ware, a gentleman in my writers' group. With his permission to print, I am sharing them.

For me, it felt delightfully delicious as if eating a great morsel of sweet-tasting chocolate. How does one describe sweet? This is so how I feel about the sensations that I felt in my body as I expressed myself in these poems. There is no word to describe sweet, but juicy is a good start.

Enjoy *Sensual Kissing Game*, *Sensual Seduction*, and *You Like It, Don't You?*

SENSUAL KISSING GAME

Where are those chocolate lips when I need them?

I'm trying to receive them

Have them bounce off mine, then come back

My tongue can see through the gasp you take

My tempted palms are on your waist

Indecisive over what to investigate

Shall your hands dance across my face

Or rest on my shoulders?

I need your lips on mine before tonight is over

I laugh as you tease, standing still, if you please

Red lipsticks on the curve of your smile

My chocolate lips leaving trails of melted honey

Sugary sweet lips to lips, tongue to tongue,
cheeks to cheeks

Your tempted palms on my waist, trailing
to my backside, pulling me close

As our slow grind begins in time and space at a
rhythm of your hand caressing my face

And your chocolate lips touch
mine before the night is over

The clock struck twelve, but
it ain't time to lay down

My tongue is in your cheek, but the
name of the game is not to play now

Grinding, our bodies flirting

Tongues wrestle, the battles urgent

Your hands pull me closer like my soul
is what your heart is deserving

I shall give you a serving once
my lips take a detour

Peppering your jawline galore

May my tongue's stroll up and down
your left ear tempt you to soar

Pull me to the couch (only if you want more)

I'd much rather stand for a little while longer

This game of sensual tantra eyes
to eyes, lips to lips,

Hands on my hips as you caress my cheeks

Tears flow as the intimacy of connection
is strong as your erection

I feel grinding as our bodies flirt

I feel peace in the sensual touch of your lips

Creating a waterfall as it spills over

Healing my hurts

Tears flow from the touch of your lips

Who knew the intimacy of kisses,
sensual kisses, your kisses

Would be the wind beneath my wings?

The chills course through my body,
proof that this kiss is more than physical

The emotional journey you take
me on is more than just a lip-lock

Your international kisses make me feel desired

The way your body melts under
my hands keep me lyrically inspired

You're tired and craving to be soothed

So all of me stands at attention, addicted
to your perfume

We beautiful humans become
a movement of illusions

Sing-song moans breathed
between us as hormones skyrocket

Wow, your breath is an
expression of your soliloquy

In moans softly, deep, deeper,
and sounds that have no name

Yet, your heartbeat speaks Morris Code, a
language my body understands just the same

My lips against your dark skin

The light of your eyes traversing
from without and within

Closed and open, opening and closing

And me

I laugh, twirl, and dance at your
addiction to my perfume … one of a kind

Pussy juice dipped in passion tasting of cherry,
butter pecan, and key lime; hmmm, so good on
your lips and mine

YOU LIKE IT, DON'T YOU?

Talkin about tit for tat

You will find your tits attacked

Bra ripped in half

Nipples moistened by my tongue

Let's see if you're digging that

While my moist fingers have some fun

In between your southern lips

Your cleavage receiving my hum

Exhaled from me

What shall you feed me? ...

You may feast on my honey dipped and dripped

Turned into cream from that loud noise

Damn! Is that your scream?

As I experience your treat

My knees wobbled, and you told me to have a seat

Legs up, legs down; shit, it didn't matter

For you stirred and played in this delicious batter

Lord you baked me down like a cake complete

All I can think of is, can we do this again?

Psshh,

You're talking like I'm done

Like I'm not gonna bless your navel with my tongue

Let my fingertips glide up your thighs

As you feel my scepter rise

To attention

His intention

Is to enter your honeypot

Stroke you deeply and rock

As you lose yourself and arch

Strokes go from gentle to hard

Firm

Steady like a piston because he yearns

To be slicked up and covered in your honey

Hmmm, baby, that is the way I like

The doctors would say I had a temperature spike

I would say they are right, but you too

My cream greases you like oil is slick

One thing you know, you are not messing with an inexperienced chick

I like what you do to me

Selfish lover … I'm not

The same way that you stirred in this honey pot

In intention calling him to attention

That beautiful black scepter on the rise, you say

Well, get ready; we may not come up for the break of day

The same way you stroke and rock as you lose yourself in the arch of my back

Well, the strokes of my hands

Play the music of millions before and after us except it is our band … our notes

Calling magic from your wand of phenomenal totality of excellence

A chef after my own heart

Been cooking my pussy from the start

I tell you to allow my lips to kiss you

You say, "Which ones?"

Hell, it doesn't matter. I am going to swallow you in every way before it is done

Then I am going to lick my lips and smile at the angels you see

While you are singing mercy merci

In English, French, and some say in tongues

Does it matter? No, not as long as you are free

SENSUAL SEDUCTION

Something about your scent

Just breathes new life in me

I must know your every wound and every joy

The other side of me

Wants you to whisper into my ear,
"I crave you inside of me!"

Both wishes can be granted excitedly

The chills you get when our convos
flow like rivers have no gaps

Flood the banks of our soul

I feel them too

It's so relaxing

After a taxing day to unwind like that

Looking like fine de Cocoa wine; ooh, I like that!

If only I can remember being hyped
for the debut of Sexual Healing

When it seemed like Marvin Gaye
had broken his ceiling

You'd find me more appealing than forbidden

And be more than flattered when I express
regret that you're not in my kitchen

Kitchen? Nah Poppie!

But we be cooking something

Stoking our conversations

Stroking our imaginations

Elevation is the goal merging
our souls into the forever

No plagiarizing the way they do it

Although done by many

We so fuckin hot we have couples
asking to get in it

We don't get down like that, but I saw the
twinkle in your eye

For me … you say

Good answer … you chose to live another day

Damn, these word games we play
have us both turned up

I crave you inside of me

Well, I shall fulfill

Make the neighbors' night go downhill

While my tongue goes out of its
way to replace the silk

Purple dress that you've adorned

On second thought, leave it on

Let me disappear under it; may
what you FEEL turn you on

I'm learning your lady parts

As my tongue travels in different directions

As your adlibs are adding to my erection

So when you gave me your wish, in
what way do you want me inside?

Should I continue to hide or have
my optics lock with your brown eyes?

Oooohweee Poppie

Like Burger King, you say I can have it my way

The art of voyeurism with each other turns me on

While I watch you stroke yourself up, down, and
in and out

81

Finally, you leaning in going
deep throat in my mouth

Brown eyes you see until I am aroused,
then grey they be

My pleasure is to watch in your delight
until you cum like the eruption of volcano

Hot Lava flows down, and I am satisfied

As the art of voyeurism brings me to my peak
receiving you as you flow deep

Deep inside of me

You taste good

Weakness overtakes me

Until your grey returns to brown

"Take me!" you command

I shall not delay

Instead, I shall lay

Get on top and see how much you can take

Battling gravity

While my phallus probes your heavenly cavity

Your rose, so fresh, so wet, so
scintillating, with no thorns

82

I'm slamming your pelvis onto mine
until we harmoniously blast like horns

Mouths tasting each other's
chocolate like rebellious kids

Now, who's acting what age?

Our experience stays youthful

Now let me surprise you by replacing
my manhood with my tongue as
you bloom ... ohhh ...

Riding on the top like a woman
upon her black stallion

In a rhythm akin to a ritual to her God

No rebellion

Clitoris sensations rubbing and
bowing to her Lord

Praises and worship at the tone
of fire shut up in her bones

I know you can feel it

So can I

Then you switch on me

Damn your tongue feels delicious

Honey, Honey, Honey,

These words become a drum
like the beating of my heart

Fuck, that tongue has the mind
of intelligence, and it is so smart

Lips moving across me as I am
being played like a flute

Strumming me like the fingers
softly like the Luther Vandross song

Tute tute tute

Hear my salute to you

I scream in release

You scream ambition

And it echoes into my soul

Clitoris on the tip of my tongue

But your legacy, I shall not forget

Nor your taste

My mouth races to catch every drop

Sucking the last remnant of honey from you

Before releasing with a manly "pop"

I promised to snatch your soul

Not just in ways carnal

I aim to discover emotions and lessons you
learned, entrenched within

The confines of your melanated skin

And Eartha Kitt legs

Care to join me in the shower or skip to the eggs?

Baby, I am a mirror reflection of us

Our melanated skin, a representation of

Ambition, wisdom, poise, and king/queen statue

We rise as the rapture when God
comes for His/Her people

You in your ejaculation, and me in my orgasm

Both reaching the epiphany
of heights of a towering climax

Unspoken words of love, an
uncompleted story of you and me

You ask the question of water, another baptism
that cleanses us for the next round

Baby, we can do both cleanse and eat,
for we stand on holy ground

Sanctimonious right righteous thinking

A spiritual journey we are on

As we bend time and live our spiritual truth

Taking ourselves in the future and
reminiscent of our youth

Both leading us to where we are
now and where we are going

As we stare into the windows of our souls

Remembering a long time ago of love
unthawing our cold hearts

Both ending relationships that fell apart

Then we fell into each other, giving
us a brand new start

I desire it all

Will you wash my back and
fuck me in the shower stall?

Eat me all over again

You say our eggs will get cold

I say not a chance

The dance of proportional grace and
mercy will flame the heat on the stove

Changing the context from
scrambled to hardboiled eggs

We have succeeded in our dance

Of love reunited

CHAPTER 7:

SHORT STORIES II

* * * * * *

I have included a miniature story and a short story as a bonus.

WE MET IN PARIS

I was out for late-night stroll, and I stopped at a cafe. As I sat staring at the moon, you stopped and said "Beautiful." I said, "She really is." I felt you staring. You looked me in my eyes and said, "She truly is." They say our eyes are the windows to our soul. I saw fire, ice, water, and air in yours ... the elements of a fierce warrior. Your spirit called to me. Curiosity propelled me forward. I invited you to have a seat. We shared our hearts, which felt like poetry in motion. We left the cafe holding hands, dancing in step with the rhythm of more conversation. I let you lead me. We ended up at your place. Reaching over to kiss you ... damn, I woke up.

WALKING INTO MY DESTINY

I'm on my way to the airport, thinking about my time in Paris and those beautiful beaches. Nothing can get me down, not even the 10 degrees below zero that feels like 50 degrees below in my jalopy, nor the fact that I will leave 'Him' in a tow-away zone because I do not have the money to park. I am not sure if I am returning anyway. He has given me some of the best rides of my life and rocked my world. I have seen my reflection through his eyes. Everything has a season. He has warmed my ass and allowed me to lean back and relax while holding me with his strong body. Yes, ma'am, my 22-year-old car has been gracious to me. I have traveled to more places, seen my own reflection through his eyes, and learned what orgasmic living could be. I look back as I exit him. Tears flow, but I know our season is over.

I look out at the water, and I barely see it as I look at the chocolate drops to my left and my right. It is so many of them, and I chuckle and think I can have them all, but I have to start with one. That task was taken out of my hands when a caramel brother made eye contact with me. His gaze felt like a warm touch of wind, a decadent breeze, had brushed against me. He glided over to me. At least it felt that way. One minute he was standing afar, and the next right beside me. He tells me his name is Todd. He must have seen my smirk as I think in my head, *What kind of name is that for a melanated man?* He seems to read my thoughts and says "My name is fuck your brains out" before he laughs and says, "My friends call me Dominique, but you can call me whatever you like as long as I can spend time with you."

Dominique asks if I would like something to drink, and I say, "Water with lemon." I thought he was going to give me a smart come back like a virgin for a virgin, but he did not. When he returned, he had two glasses of water with lemons. Of course, I wondered what his deal was. He drinks wine, but it wasn't a necessity for him. We spend the next couple of hours laughing and talking. He has me in stitches as he talks about the pranks he and his brother played on each other. He asks me my story. I was trying to think of something to say when he said, "Be, just be you." By the time we had laughed and talked all day and played in the water and slept for play of such an intimate nature had been exacted upon mind, heart, body, and soul each had been penetrated.

We agreed to meet for dinner after which we decided to take a walk on the beach. My body was humming from earlier, and Dominique was in tune with it, playing his own instrument. We stopped at the beach. I could feel his imprint in my hand as he looked at me at questioned if he could kiss me. I nodded yes. He understood my yes surpassed a kiss. He looked again to inquire if I was sure. I said yes but did not recognize my own voice. I began to clear it. He laid his coat down and undressed me under the moon, then himself. He played my body with his lips like it was a flute. By the time he kissed down my stomach and blew between the apex of my thighs, I climaxed so hard. He asked me if I was OK, and I said yes. Hell no, I am not OK.

I straddled him sensitive but determined to bring him the joy he brought to me through his touch and his voice. As I rode him with my two yoni eggs inside and used the art of clutching him so tight he may as well had been with a virgin—his sounds where so sacred that the night and the ocean stood still to pay homage to the man and woman lying before them. I spoke into his soul in silence, chanting words of power, sensual words, and words of praises while gazing into his eyes seeing. Later, he told me his soul felt like it was taking flight. That was 5 years ago. My husband is feeding me chocolate while rubbing my feet, saying, "Tresa to earth." I sit up and realize I am more in love with this man than ever before. I am a worshiped woman.

DEDICATED TO THE VOICE OF MY INNER GURU

AT PEACE

I am an amazing girl

Living life in a swirl

Of many flavors

Vanilla, chocolate, and strawberry

There is no one like me

I am all three

I am an individual who loves herself

ACKNOWLEDGMENT

I would like to acknowledge some of the women on my journey, who have truly impacted my life. To my mentors, coaches, big sisters, or a combination and in some cases all three. Dr. Aikyna Finch, I will always be grateful that you saw me and called me forth. Your words have become my voice when I'm afraid. "Stop hiding. You have a greater purpose." Janine Ingram, your fearlessness in telling me the truth and thus said Spirit supported me in getting my book cover completed and being free and truly naked. You were my right angel when Dr. Finch was my left. Latonia Taylor; going through your rites of passage program changed my life, but not before Mother Wisdom through you required I give everything and then some. Thema Azize Serwa, you planted and cultivated the seed "the story I tell, I get to live." I am deeply grateful I heard you.

Spirit Halima, because of you, I identify as a worshipped woman. I own my birthright. Dannie Stillwell, whew, you taught me the power my sensuality held. Girrrllll, I know you had no idea what you unleashed, but I am forever grateful. Rev. Shaheerah Stephens, one of the most profound lessons I learned from you was about integrity. I do my best to live in integrity and understand answers are not just answers. Dr. Stephanie Coleman, thank you for planting the seed of money consciousness in me. They are rooting, and your unconditional love and ability to be non-judgmental when you knew I was not ready was not lost on me. Dr. Vikki, your wisdom regarding this book is already opening doors for me to plant my feet.

Pearlette Ramos, Diana Cross, Tyscka Roper, Rhonda Byrd (twin), Enid Carter Cutchins, and Colette Estes, thank you for being the big sisters that nurtured me. You were the voice of reason and wisdom. I am a better woman because of all of you. Cathy Iverson, thank you for your raw truth. This is not a dress rehearsal. Everything that is happening, I'm experiencing it now. Your words were the hand I needed that day as I wrestled with inward evolution), and A Night on the Town in Our PJs.

Tresa is a visionary, life coach, author, speaker, and poet. She is an Usui Reiki I practitioner and a certified Womb practitioner through the Womb Sauna University. Tresa is a lifelong learner who says that she will continue to further her education that ignites her core passion to empower women who are on their healing journey.

Tresa loves to read and exercise, particularly to run; spend time with her 9 grandchildren, family, friends, and with her sister tribe. She has a secret desire to learn to belly dance and pole dance.

Feel free to stay connected with Tresa Simmons on social media at:

http://www.bohemiangoddess.live
https://www.facebook.com/tresa.simmons
Uniquelybrilliant2@gmail.com
TresaSimmons@LinkedIn.com
Uniquelybrillianttwo@Instagram.com